HEALING

WITH TIME

AND LOVE:

A Guide

For Visiting The Elderly

Sister Patricia Murphy, O.L.V.M.

This monograph
is published by
The Ethel Percy Andrus Gerontology Center
University of Southern California
Los Angeles, California 90007

RICHARD H. DAVIS, Ph.D.
Director of Publications and Media Projects

THE UNIVERSITY OF SOUTHERN CALIFORNIA PRESS
ISBN 0-88474-092-7
Library of Congress Card Catalog Number 79-66983

Managing Editor: Richard Bohen
Editorial Assistant: Jean Rarig

Preface

There never has been a time when caring people have not been concerned with those sick and frail elderly persons who are confined at home or in long term care institutions. There never has been a time when there have been so many elderly people who find themselves cut off from the community.

People who see with the eye of the heart are eager to diminish the isolation and loneliness that can accompany frailness and illness in the elderly. Special kinds of understanding are important, and there is new research to incorporate. This guidebook provides basic aids for friendly visitors, nursing home ombudsmen, nursing home personnel, and families and friends of the sick and frail elderly.

Until the warmth of genuine human caring breathes life into a relationship, all the information and statistics contained in this guide remain simply facts. Surpassing all the factual knowledge about our sick and frail elderly is the significance of the *person*, whose mystery can be touched only by another human being—another human being who treasures his or her own uniqueness, and who can relate to others with that same cherishing respect. Not even the desperate need charitable overtures. Because the elderly sick are somewhat captive, friendly visitors may need to evaluate regularly their motivations.

Nothing is quite so precious as moments shared between people who are continually discovering how meaningful they are to each other. If I am important and bring something unique to another's life, or will be missed because of that someone's perception of me, then I am assured of my value. My self-esteem increases! Simply breathing becomes worthwhile! Let us enable each other to live alive until we draw our last breath.

Sister Patricia Murphy, O.L.V.M.
Santa Monica, California
June 1979

Contents

Acknowledgments

Grateful thanks to the Santa Monica, California, Westside Ecumenical Conference Visitation Ministry, who made the need for such a guide clear and then empowered and inspired me to write it; to the Pacific Palisades, California, Rotary Club, who sponsored the first copies and espoused the idea with heart and feeling; and to Reverend Robert Nunn, who saw to it that the guide made "the last mile."

Introduction 1

YOU Are Your Best Gift

Nothing in this life can compare with the gift of self. For old persons in health care institutions, "real presence" is a rarity. A friendly visitor brings this best gift with an open heart. Time and love mean more than pills and doctors.

> The emptiness of the past and the future can never be filled with words but only by the presence of a man. Because only then can the hope be born that there might be at least one exception to the "nobody and nothing" of his complaint—a hope that will make him whisper, "Maybe, after all, someone is waiting for me."[1]

You have wept, ached, longed, and waited. You have endured pain, isolation, loss, failure, and uselessness. Your experience gives you a basic quality as a visitor. You are a "wounded healer."

1. Nouwen, H. J. M. *The Wounded Healer: Ministry in Contemporary Society.* Garden City, N. Y.: Doubleday & Co., Inc., © 1972, p. 65.

1

After so much stress on the necessity of a leader to prevent his own personal feelings and attitudes from interfering in a helping relationship . . . it seems necessary to re-establish the basic principle that no one can help anyone without becoming involved, without entering with his whole person into the painful situation, without taking the risk of becoming hurt, wounded or even destroyed in the process. The beginning and the end of all Christian leadership is to give your life for others. Thinking about martyrdom can be an escape unless we realize that real martyrdom means a witness that starts with the willingness to cry with those who cry, laugh with those who laugh, and to make one's own painful and joyful experiences available as sources of clarification and understanding. . . . The great illusion of leadership is to think that man can be led out of the desert by someone who has never been there.[2]

Aging is the turning of the wheel, the gradual fulfillment of the life cycle. . . . Aging does not need to be hidden or denied, but can be understood, affirmed, and experienced as a process of growth by which the mystery of life is slowly revealed to us.[3]

2. Nouwen, H. J. M., *The Wounded Healer: Ministry in Contemporary Society*. Garden City, N. Y.: Doubleday & Co., Inc., © 1972, pp. 72–73.

3. Nouwen, H. J. M., & Gaffney, W. J. *Aging: The Fulfillment of Life*. Garden City, N. Y.: Doubleday & Co., Inc., © 1974; Image Books edition, 1976.

Facts on Aging—A Short Quiz[4]

T F 1. The majority of persons past age 65 are senile, have defective memory, are disoriented.

T F 2. Older persons are not treatable because their mental conditions are inevitable and irreversible.

T F 3. Most older persons have no interest in, or capacity for sexual relations.

T F 4. All five senses tend to decline in old age.

T F 5. Lung capacity tends to decline in old age.

T F 6. The majority of old people feel miserable all the time.

T F 7. Physical strength tends to decline in old age.

T F 8. At least one tenth of the aged are living in long-stay institutions (nursing homes, homes for the aged, mental institutions).

T F 9. Most old people are set in their ways and unable to change.

T F 10. Old people usually take longer to learn something new.

T F 11. The reaction of most old people tends to be slower than that of younger people.

T F 12. In general, most old people are pretty much alike.

T F 13. The majority of old people are socially isolated and lonely.

4. Palmore, E. Facts on Aging: A Short Quiz. *The Gerontologist* 1977, *17*(4), 315–320. Some questions from course work at University of California, Berkeley, n.d.

T F 14. Over 15% of the U.S. population are now age 65 and older.

T F 15. Most medical practitioners tend to give the aged low priority.

T F 16. The majority of older people have incomes below the poverty level.

T F 17. Older people tend to become more religious as they age.

T F 18. The majority of older people are seldom irritated or angry.

T F 19. There are approximately four times as many widows as widowers.

T F 20. The health and socioeconomic status of older people (compared to younger people) in the year 2000 will probably be the same as now.

T F 21. Achievement in various scientific, artistic and creative fields is highest in younger years and steadily decreases.

T F 22. Most elderly people can expect retirement to reduce their incomes by 50% or more.

T F 23. The elderly are more inclined to solve their problems on the basis of past experience or solutions rather than experimenting with new ones.

T F 24. With regard to mental functioning, many declines experienced by the elderly are not apparent except under stress conditions.

T F 25. Though older people often express awareness of death in conversations they are not fearful of it.

T F 26. People naturally recognize when they are old.

T F 27. T.V. watching is more of a leisure pursuit for the elderly than for any other age-range.

Facts on Aging Answer Sheet

1. F Only about 10% of persons aged 65 and older are institutionalized as a result of psychiatric illness. It is more difficult to get accurate estimates of the proportion with defective memories—partly because of the different types of memory defects and different methods in measuring it.

2. F It is because society considers it useless to waste time dealing with the mental and emotional problems of the aged that there is so little done.

3. F The majority have both interest in and capacity for sexual relations.

4. T Most studies agree that various aspects of vision, hearing and touch tend to decline in old age, as well as in taste and smell. Most older people fear loss of vision more than anything else.

5. T Lung capacity does tend to decline in old age.

6. F Studies show either no significant difference by age groups, or that most felt they were just as happy as when they were "young."

7. T Physical strength tends to decline in old age (muscular strength).

8. F 4.8% of persons over age 65, and 9.2% of persons over age 75 were residents in long-stay institutions.

9. F Older people do tend to become more stable in their attitudes, but most of them do change and adapt to many events that affect old age.

10. T Statistics on experiments consistently prove this.

11. T One of the best documented facts on aging —appears to be true regardless of the kind of reaction measured.

12. F There appears to be at least as much difference between older people as there is at any age level. . . . some studies show them to be less alike as they age.

13. F About two-thirds of the aged say they are never or hardly ever lonely. Most of these statistics are true about people who are mobile and who have family nearby.

14. F Only 10.3% of the population was 65 or older in 1975.

15. T Studies show that most doctors, nurses, occupational therapy and psychiatric personnel tend to believe the negative stereotypes about the aged and prefer to work with any other age range.

16. F The majority of elderly people have incomes well above the poverty level.

17. F The present generation of older people tends to be more religious than the younger generation—this appears to be an environmental difference rather than an age difference.

18. T Studies show that over one-half of the aged said they are never or hardly ever irritated, and this percentage increased to two-thirds after age 80.

19. T Wars, susceptibility to heart attacks and other diseases are causes.
20. F It will probably be much higher. By 2000 the gaps in health, income, occupation and education will be substantially less.
21. F There are a number of case histories to prove this false. Most creative endeavors better with maturity.
22 T That's the facts.
23. T Life's experiences, and working solutions or failures of the past guide older persons.
24. T The loss of a mate, or discovery of serious illness, or economic misadventures will often highlight existing problems.
25. T Studies show that they are not fearful of the coming of death, but would like to be more free to talk about it.
26. F Generally people recognize when SOMEONE ELSE is old—not themselves.
27. F Children watch far more T.V. than older persons.

2 The Convalescent Home[1]

What Is It?

Taken at face value, it is a place where people convalesce. That is partly true. It is also true that for many patients it is their last home on earth. It is part hospital, where ailments are treated, and it is part home, where people may live from one to seven years before they die.

Who Lives There?

The average age of people in convalescent homes is eighty-three, although there are always some younger patients suffering from multiple sclerosis, muscular dystrophy, and cancer.

Most patients have some inhibiting illness that makes it impossible for them to live by themselves or

1. Some of the following is applicable to board-and-care facilities and retirement hotels.

in some other group setting. Their families are unable to care for them at home any longer, or they have no family at all.

Many patients have bones on the mend and need the daily therapy offered by convalescent homes.

Some patients are confused and forgetful. They are not senile, but they don't always know where they are or what happened yesterday. These people often do not have serious illnesses, but their confusion makes it dangerous for them to be on their own. They need protective custody.

Every convalescent home has a few senile people who are confused about everything. They are not sure who they are, why they are there, and cannot carry on a conversation that makes sense to the listener.

What Do You See?

Your first introduction to a convalescent home can be very upsetting. People in all forms of dress are often crowded near the door so they can be where the action is. Their eyes seem to search for a sign of life meant for them—a smile, a warm word, a handshake. They often seem without animation and quite forlorn. Because most convalescent homes have incontinent patients, there is often a distinct odor that no chemical firm has been able to solve. If you walk down the hallways you will see patients sitting idle or slumped in their chairs asleep. Often the TVs are on, but few really watch them. One or two sick patients may be moaning in pain; senile patients may call out for help, not always knowing what for.

Is It Always Like This?

This view could frighten anyone away. But it is not the whole picture. Every convalescent home has activity programs that are geared to meet some of the social, creative, physical, spiritual, and intellectual needs of the residents. There are morning and afternoon sessions that include current events, bingo, table games, arts and crafts, church services, movies, entertainments, and parties. In addition, many facilities provide programs for the bed-bound and the room-bound. Every conceivable type of volunteer is utilized to make a more wholesome atmosphere. When patients are engaged in activities or are enjoying visitors, family, or friends, they present a whole new picture. They are smiling, more active, and alert—much like any other older person who has aches and pains to bear.

Friendly Visiting—It Makes a Difference

Visitors make such a difference in the lives of older sick people. Visitors provide the opportunity to engage in conversation about the world "outside," share happenings, revisit the past, and build friendships. Visitors are a second set of eyes for the blind person, the active limbs for an arthritic person, the patient speaker for those going deaf, and the companion for those who have few relatives or friends. The more people who are active in caring for these sick men and women in health care institutions, the fewer people we will see lined up in foyers and hallways desperately looking for a friendly face.

But It Is an Institution

This is a convalescent home, and has rules for the better ordering of life within its walls. It is an integral part of the responsibility of each visitor to become acquainted with these rules, and in addition to acquire a sixth sense which allows him to get along with patients and staff alike.

3 The Elderly Resident

A Profile of the Elderly Person in a Convalescent Setting

Older persons suffer any number of a series of losses as they age. There is often the loss of a mate and many dear friends through death. Children may have moved away or grown away. Economic sufficiency is a loss suffered by many aging persons, with little opportunity to alter that situation. Loss of physical adeptness keeps the aging persons from doing some of the things that were a source of joy and satisfaction in their younger years. Most older persons are retirees, often with a bewildering sense of loss and an insecurity about their worth and value in this action/business-oriented society.

When an older person needs the facilities of a board-and-care or convalescent home, these losses are compounded. Where before, older persons could at least direct their own lives, now they have to follow the regime of the institution. Even such a simple daily routine as a morning cup of coffee at the moment of wakening is no longer possible. Any institution has problems with privacy, and some persons find the lack of privacy the ultimate indignity. Surroundings are no longer familiar, type of food is changed, and the people that crowd their days are strangers.

Institutional life is not conducive to rosy dreams of retirement and happy last years. It is expensive, and funds are soon depleted. Someone else takes over the management of financial affairs. One doesn't even sign one's own checks very often. It is hard to feel human and loved and valuable when such a setting is so different from one's dreams. Yet, incredibly enough, most of the residents in institutional care show a great deal of courage as they greet each day and each friendly face that comes their way. More than most, these people are incredibly appreciative of any kindness and thoughtfulness. They have the will and the capacity to live worthwhile lives—yes, even in this setting. But they cannot do it alone.

Those people who react adversely to institutional settings and turn apathetic and unresponsive are often the ones who need most the respectful, caring presence of a friendly visitor. Patients with pathological diseases that produce confusion, disorientation, or "senility" are still capable of relating to people on the heart level. Having someone truly appreciate them "where they are" often releases unsuspected resources.

Most doctors who deal with the elderly agree that loneliness is the greatest of their problems. It is well documented that time and love do more for the elderly sick than medicine. So it is that we invite the visitor to be the physician of time and love.

Tips for Families

Before the need for a long term care facility. Much of the unhappiness that occurs within a family when a loved one is admitted to a nursing home might have been diminished if there had been dialogue about the possibility long before such a move became necessary. One research study tells us that one out of every twenty-five people will spend some time in a nursing home. In order that the experience may be as whole-some as possible, it is important to have talked about the possibility, discussed the anxieties, looked to ways these could be less stressful, and decided that it would be possible not only to survive such a move, but to do well in the new location. Such a positive attitude could cut the average length of stay in half.

Before placement. Most states have guides for choosing the best nursing home. These are often un-realistic under existing circumstances. Often so little bed space is available that families must take what they can get. *If there is time to look around:*

1. Look for personnel at as many levels of care as possible, and speak with them. If they are friendly and helpful before you place someone, they are likely to have those characteristics most of the time. Plea-sant caregiving personnel are essential to the success of the experience; one can better do without some of the frills and expensive decor.

2. Check on the state of cleanliness in the rooms and general areas. Do this more than once and at dif-ferent times of the day. Understandably, odors can arise at certain times, but this should not be a general condition.

3. Notice the grooming of the residents. If hair, nails, and clothes are reasonably clean, it is a very good sign that individual attention is being given on a regular basis.

4. Look for pleasant, well lighted, well ventilated environments.

5. Arrive at mealtime. See whether the food is appetizing. Ask the residents if they like what they are eating. (Remember, though, that criticism of institutional food is a survival tactic.) Check to see how assistance in eating is provided for those who need it, and how soon they are helped.

6. Check the activity program schedule, which should be posted. Even though you feel your loved one does not need that kind of program, you can estimate the attention to psychosocial needs by the variety and time-plan of the activity program available.

7. Results of the most recent Health Department inspection are supposed to be posted in an accessible place. The number of citations is sometimes a sign of the kind of performance of a facility, but the *content* of the citations is generally more informative. Do this as unobtrusively as possible. Too much checking makes staff cautious about accepting a patient who is related to the questioner.

After placement.

Remember that your loved one remains pretty much the same person as before admission, with the same needs, habits, likes, and dislikes. Maintain the type of relationship you have had previously as much as possible.

Remember that there will be a need for adjustment time. There will be a certain amount of anger, resentment, fear, and insecurity with which the loved one will have to deal. Patients may not sleep well for a while. They may alter their eating patterns. They may frequently ask to be taken home. During this time they will need understanding, patience, and love shown in visible ways.

Remember that you too need time to adjust to this situation. You will have unfinished feelings that will affect the quality and frequency of your visits. Give yourself time. Find one of the professionals at the facility with whom you feel you can talk, and share your feelings. If there is a social service person, be sure to get in touch.

Remember that although your loved one will need the reassurance of your visits, too frequent and too lengthy visits can harm the patient's capacity to adapt to the situation, to find friends, or to reflect on what is taking place. Some residents spend their entire time sitting on the edge of their chair by the door waiting for family, when participation in the nursing home's events would bring new friendships and fulfill the need for social interaction. Check with the nursing staff concerning the optimum frequency of visits that would best benefit your loved one.

Remember that you are permitted, as space allows, to bring in a few of the patient's personal effects. This often facilitates adjustment. Bring pictures of family and friends, and place them in prominent spots.

Remember that you may be able to secure permission to take your loved one out of the facility. A nice meal in a restaurant will do wonders for a resident's morale. Shopping for little necessities keeps one in touch with the world and gives a feeling of being in charge. Such excursions can be done by wheelchair if the resident is unable to walk about.

Remember that socializing while eating is a very important part of life. Bring your lunch and share it with your loved one. Bring a picnic with foods your loved one can eat (check with nursing). Have a crystal, silver, and flower setting for the dinner!

Remember that you can assist in the care of your loved one. However, be aware that if you do this on a regular basis, the staff may come to expect it—and you may find them neglecting the tasks you usually do when you are absent.

Remember that the facility generally provides washing services—institutional laundry service, however, which is hard on clothes. Keep on hand a supply of inexpensive clothes that can't be damaged easily. Clothes sometimes mysteriously disappear. Some families prefer to do the laundering of clothes themselves.

Remember that you can have privacy for your visits. You may have to ask for a special room, but do not hesitate. Remind your loved one to ask for such a space if there is a desire to talk with someone in privacy.

Remember that we all need people to talk with. When uprooted from familiar surroundings, one feels this need even more strongly. Families often believe they must provide a private room for their loved one. While this choice may make the *family* feel better, patients' physical and emotional states are frequently better if they have roommates. If a roommate seems incompatible, you can request a transfer; you may have to wait a while, but if the change seems warranted and important, continue to request the transfer.

Remember that you can inquire as to nurses' notes, doctors' orders, weight loss or gain, elimination, and other important areas. Most often the desk nurse will be glad to inform you. It is wise to choose a time when the activities at the nurses' desk are slow. You may need to make an appointment, or you may find that a phone call is as satisfactory as trying to talk to the personnel while you are there.

Remember that staff persons need positive feedback just as you do in your work. I encourage families to spend a brief part of every visit being friendly with the staff personnel. This doesn't mean talking away their time, but a short conversation, frequent thanks for work well done, and genuine appreciation will do much to insure better care for your loved one and more acceptance of your need to talk when it becomes necessary.

Remember that you can join forces with other families and form a family council. It helps to know others who are in a similar situation and who can share your concerns and anxieties. Perhaps between you, solutions to making life in the facility more bearable may emerge. Facilities are likewise being encouraged to develop residents' councils as well, so residents can be involved in their own care and in the functioning of their environment.

Ombudsman Programs. Most states have an ombudsman program which provides troubleshooting services for consumers of nursing home industry services. These ombudsmen are available to help either you or the resident obtain necessary and proper services while receiving long term care. The State Department of Aging is the place to inquire.

Patients' Rights[1]

Just by fact of being human, we have certain rights. These rights are built on the basics that are

1. Adapted from *Skilled Nursing Facilities Regulations*, California Administrative Code Title 22, Division 5, Chapter 3.

needed to live in dignity. Residents in long term care facilities have *human rights* as well as *special rights* demanded by the transaction of trust and the payment of fees. There are times when any of us can give way on our rights because we feel something more is to be gained by not insisting on them. However, that is our choice. Residents in long term care should be aware of their rights. Family and friends can do much to insure them. These rights are protected by state Departments of Health (see each state's administrative code for specifics.)

Each patient admitted to a nursing home has a right to:

Be fully informed of his rights, and of the facility's rules

Be fully informed of the services available and of all charges

Be fully informed by his physician of his medical condition; to have the opportunity to participate in the planning of his medical treatment; to be informed of the medical consequences of refusal for treatment; and the right to refuse to participate in experimental research

Be transferred or discharged only for medical reasons, or for his welfare or for that of other residents, or for non-payment; he has a right to be given reasonable advance notice

Manage his personal affairs, or be given quarterly accounting of transactions made on his behalf if the facility accepts this responsibility

Be free from mental and physical abuse, from chemical and (except for emergencies) physical restraints unless authorized in writing by the physician

Be assured of confidentiality regarding medical
 records
Be treated with dignity and respect, including
 privacy in treatment and in care for physical
 needs
Associate and communicate privately with persons of his choice (including clergy at any
 time)
Receive mail unopened
Retain use of personal clothing and possessions
 as space permits unless to do so would in-
 fringe on the rights of others
If married, privacy for visits of spouses, and if
 both are in the facility, to share the same
 room
Be visited at any time when condition is critical
 (unless this would be harmful to the patient's
 condition)
Have reasonable access to telephone communi-
 cation

The Visitor 4

Assets and Benefits

It has earlier been noted that every person who has suffered the pains that come with living has already a prerequisite for meeting the needs of the elderly sick. Surfacing from suffering and pain with dignity and wholeness is something we have all tried to achieve. This experience will be an invaluable aid to a visitor. Here are other assets that are important in becoming a quality visitor to the elderly sick:

It is important to like elderly people—to be aware of their value, not only in the past, but also in their present condition. They can have a perception of the essences of life that cannot be gained from a younger or healthier stance.

It is important to be able to take illnesses for what they are—a misfortune, but not a disaster. A visitor must be able to look past the disagreeable aspects of the illnesses that brought the person to a convalescent home, but not ignore them.

It is important to be able to offer the gift of unhurried time. For the hour or two of your visit, you must be as unaffected by time and pressure as possible.

It is important to be able to share yourself. Your best assets are your own person and experience. Willingness to share these is essential to establish a bridge between the patient's world and yours.

It is important to be able to face your own aging. Aging is a process we are all going through each moment, but it is a temptation to hang on to a sense of our own immortality, to grasp at the belief that "this won't happen to us." If we are able to face our own aging and mortality, we will be at ease with these witnesses to it.

It is important to have a sense of humor. Laughter is one of the missing ingredients in a nursing home, yet given the chance, patients respond to humor easily; it lightens their burdens.

It is important to be able to recognize the value of the convalescent home for some people. It will be difficult for the people you visit to maintain a sense of dignity in their setting if they sense that you can see no possible good in it. Every circumstance has some good in it and some value to be discovered. Although our environment definitely affects us, it does not make us.

It is important to be able to work with the staff in a convalescent home. Most homes work hard at being good places to be. They count on your support and cooperation. When difficulties arise, there are ways of handling them that are beneficial to the patient and to the home.

Meeting the Convalescent Home Resident

Many people wonder how you go about meeting a long term care resident who would appreciate and benefit from your friendship. You can just walk up to a nursing home and say, "Do you need me?" You might be surprised to hear someone say, "Well, I don't think so." Usually the people at the desk do not deal with volunteers or know how to put them in touch with the right people. If you do not know of a group in the facility with a visiting program, the person to see is the Activity Director. The Activity Director is responsible for the social integration and outreach of the residents, and is usually extremely grateful to know that you want to help.

The Activity Director (or the Volunteer Director) will want to get to know you, know about your hobbies, talents, and interests so that you can be matched up with someone who will relate well to you. The Activity Director can give you a brief medical history and personality profile for each of the individuals you will visit; the Activity Director also is the first person to question when something seems wrong or changed in the behavior of your residents. The Activity Director is the person to contact if you do not understand some of the procedures in the facility. If you visit at times when the Activity Director is absent, it is a good idea to telephone to talk about the people you have taken into your friendship. Don't let worries or wondering build up, as this affects the quality of your visiting and has a great deal of effect on your endurance.

The initial meeting with your new friend will be no easier nor more difficult than a meeting with anyone for the first time. You have already made many relationships over the years, so you already know what makes it easy to reach someone and how to get conversations started and flowing. Remember, the resident may have been isolated for a long time or unpracticed in the art of conversation. You may have to

"prime the pump." Start talking about things you
see around you—pictures, if any, hair style, clothing.
Share yourself, your family, the kind of day you have
had. Try using some of the questions in the "Life
Review/Reminiscence" section of this guidebook.

Make it a point to become more knowledgeable
about aging in general and the sick and frail elderly
in particular. Every city, or at least every county, has
information and programs devoted to the elderly
which are available to the public. Check with the
Area Agency on Aging, the Department of Aging, the
Department of Senior Citizens' Affairs, and your
senators' and congressmen's offices.

Life Review/Reminiscence

Life review/reminiscence is a good therapeutic
approach to older persons. Doctors, psychiatrists, and
social workers are beginning to recognize its worth,
not just for recalling "the good old days," but for the
therapy of remembering times when the individual
was a person in good standing with peers and society.
Following are some questions used in life review
therapy:

Birthplace.   Where were you born? Were your par-
    parents born there?
Grandparents.   What can you remember about your
    grandparents? Where were they born? What did
    they do?
Parents—Mother.   What was your mother like? Was
    she a good cook? What was one of her best
    dishes?

Parents—Father. What kind of work did your father do? What did he like to do best?

Religion. What was the role of religion in your family?

Neighborhood. What do you remember about the town where you grew up? What do you remember about your school—your favorite teachers, and the subjects you liked best?

Growing Up. How did you spend your summers? Did you have any hobbies, favorite songs, or sports? What were some of the customs? Was it different for a boy than a girl?

Moves. When did you first move from home? Where did you move to, and what effect did it have on you?

Work. What kind of work did you do? What wages were you paid? What did you buy with your first check?

Entertainment. What did you adults do for fun? What were your favorite radio programs and movies?

What do you remember about

World War I	Prohibition
World War II	The Depression
The Twenties	McCarthy hearings

What are your feelings regarding

Money	Humor
Women's liberation	Family
Health	Today's youth
Sex	

Politics. Who was the first president you voted for? Who was your favorite president, and why? Who are some of the men and women you admire most?

Philosophy of Life.   What have been some of the
    most significant changes in your lifetime? Any
    single life event that stands out as most impor-
    tant? If you could re-live any day in your life,
    what would that be? What message would you
    like to pass on to your children? To the world?
    How do you feel about the direction your life has
    taken?

The present also provides valuable topics for conversations. The news items of the day are of interest
to older people—not murders, rapes, and robberies,
but news of the wider world that is shaping our
tomorrows.

Your life provides interesting conversation topics.
While it is important to let your new friend talk about
himself, it will be a one-sided relationship if you don't
share your own life in all its unfinished state. Feel free
to describe events you have been to, the season of the
year, clothes you have bought, family experiences,
your job or volunteer work, your hobbies, and things
of interest you have read. Whatever you share,
describe it vividly, taking the resident right along
with you.

Toward Effective Visits

Remember your most valuable asset—yourself—
and share from that wealth.

Remember your purpose—to provide a friendly
relationship for sick elderly people who have few personal contacts.

Remember your new friends need to have a personal someone who is cheerful and who really cares
about them in a creative way.

Remember that this is a person with a long history of successes and defeats, of happy memories and dreaded rememberings, of up days and down days—and that this person in every way is much like you.

Remember to confer on this patient, no matter how sick or feeble, all the rights and privileges of friendship—the right to warm regard, the right to honor for accomplishments, the right to confidentiality, the right to honesty, the right to expect commitment, the privilege of loving you back.

Remember the importance of allowing your new friend to do for you, to give something to you, if it be only so simple a thing as holding your purse for you or marking a spot in a book.

Remember how important it is to have someone safe to gripe with. Allow your friend to complain, take him or her seriously; then set out to make the visit a positive experience.

Remember how much you value a good listener, and bestow this gift on your elderly friend. Effective listening is often its own remedy for hurts.

Recall that often when you are talking you want people to look past the words you are saying to how you are feeling about the subject.

Remember that people in institutions often develop fears and anxious feelings about what is going to happen to them. Living one day at a time well is something you also try to do. Share your own experiences. Find ways of stemming the tide of anxiousness.

Remember that in almost all cases it is better to affirm what is right. Gently stating the truth always helps older confused people to have at least one source of stability.

Remember that your friend will sometimes be depressed or confused. This is an embarrassing time, and sometimes it is best to make the visit short after somehow letting them know that it is alright to have "dog days."

Remember that the things which motivate your life are not necessarily inspiration to others. More then what you say, who you are will communicate your values and your faith.

Remember also that we often like to be invited to pray, to talk about eternal realities: death, the purpose of life, the purpose of suffering, etc. Ask your friend if he or she is interested in discussing these things, and if he or she would like to pray.

Dealing with Problems

There are bound to be occasions when the visitor is upset or perplexed about proceedings in a long term care facility, especially in the beginning. How the visitor handles problems will deeply affect how he or she is accepted by the facility.

1. Assume that the facility is doing the right thing under the circumstances and that you are far from knowledgeable about the entire situation.

2. Inquire of the activity director either personally or by phone about the incident, indicating your willingness to learn the idiosyncrasies of institutional life.

3. If the response is not satisfactory, get in touch with the director of the program. This will assure that you have taken all reasonable methods to inform yourself.

4. The next step is to approach the administrator with the problem. The director will guide you in this process, and perhaps accompany you.

5. Serious problems that go unresolved should

be processed through an advocacy or ombudsman group. If there is no ombudsman program, the next step would be to inform the state health inspectors.

Most facilities welcome knowledgeable criticism. It is to their advantage to correct problems before they come to public attention.

Every visitor should spend a fraction of the time visiting getting to know the administrative personnel and nursing staff. When visitors indicate real caring for the welfare of the staff, an atmosphere of trust emerges which will create receptiveness to questions and requests for attention to the residents.

The Visitor's Accomplices

It is a natural impulse to want to take small gift items to your new friend, and the residents appreciate such thoughtfulness. Generally speaking, there is no need to check with the nursing station on items that are inedible. It is always a good idea to mark the person's name clearly in indelible ink so there will be less danger of it being lost or stolen.

Each convalescent home has its own regulations regarding the admittance of food from outside sources. Strictly speaking, it is not recommended; however, most facilities have found a humane way of handling this problem: they require that all food items be checked at the desk. Since you may not know when a patient has had a diet change, it is always best to ask about introducing a food item.

When food items are given the green light by the facility, they must always be put in a covered container unless they are to be consumed immediately. No food is allowed to lie loosely in drawers. Save convenient containers for this purpose.

Always remember that YOU are your best gift. It is easy for us to hide behind our gifts in a way that saves us from having to share a part of ourselves. We must be careful not to let our gifts attempt what time and love alone can do.

SUGGESTIONS FOR GIFTS.

Refreshments (small amounts)

Homemade cookies, cakes, etc.
Chocolate bars, candies
Small jars of jam
Ice cream, other than vanilla
Fresh fruit, washed
Dried fruit

Other

Tightly covered tin box for goodies
Kleenex
Writing paper
Hand cream, toiletries, "Wash and Dry" packets
Toothpaste, soap
Books
Flowers and plants
Small mirrors
Bedside games
Pictures
Small shopping bag; utility bag

HELPS FROM THE BIBLE.

Is your friend

Tired?   Read Psalm 95.1–7; Matthew 11
Tense?   Read Psalm 91; James 5.7–11
Worried?   Read Psalm 46; Matthew 6
Discouraged?   Read Psalms 23, 42, 43
Frustrated?   Read Psalms 40, 90; Hebrews 12; Matthew 6.25–34; Philippians 4.8–13
Depressed?   Read Psalms 34, 71; Isaiah 40

Jealous?   Read Psalm 49; James 3

Bored?   Read 2 Kings 5; Job 38; Psalms 103,104; Ephesians 3

Bereaved?   Read 1 Corinthians 15; 1 Thessalonians 4.13–5.28; Revelations 21, 22

Bearing a grudge?   Read Luke 6; 2 Corinthians 4; Ephesians 4

Staying awake nights?   Read Psalms 4, 56, 130

Lonely or fearful?   Read Psalms 27, 91; Luke 8; 1 Peter 4

Feeling rejected?   Read Colossians 1; 1 Peter 1

Sick or in pain?   Read Psalms 6, 39, 41, 67; Isaiah 26

Afraid of death?   Read John 11, 17, 20; 2 Corinthians 5; 1 John 3, Revelation 14

Anxious for loved ones?   Read Psalm 121; Luke 7

Angry with someone?   Read Matthew 18; Ephesians 4; James 4

Need forgiveness?   Read Matthew 23; Luke 15; Philemon

Weak in faith?   Read Psalms 126, 146; Hebrews 11

Does God seem far away?   Read Psalms 25, 125, 138; Luke 10; Acts 17.22–28; Jeremiah 29.11–13

Beatitudes:	Matthew 5.1–12
Great Commandment:	Luke 10.27; Matthew 22.34–40
Sermon on the Mount:	Matthew 5–7
Shepherd Psalm:	Psalm 23

—American Bible Society

Meeting Special Needs

While many of the people in long term care facilities are suffering mostly from the usual diseases, there are some illnesses that need special understanding.

Depression. Depression is not in itself usually called an illness, but it affects a great many ordinary folk and invades the lives of the elderly with a particular menace. It is one of the most common and most overlooked of the emotional illnesses of later life. Persons in long term care facilities have more than enough pressuring incidents that can cause depression: many losses, the inability to determine one's own existence, and the seeming hopelessness of the debilitating diseases and illnesses that affect people in later life. Many doctors consider depression one of the major causes of most of the illnesses that elderly people bring to their attention.

Some depressions reverse themselves without any outside help. The normal tendency of the human system is to heal itself. But when this does occur, it is usually because of the aid that comes from the fidelity and caring of good friends. When the righting does not come of itself, it is even more important for the visitor to be understanding and to support the older person who suffers from depression.

Some of the symptoms of depression are depressed mood, chronic sadness, change in gait or posture, loss of weight, insomnia, chronic physical complaints, lack of energy, constipation; feeling of hopelessness, helplessness, and worthlessness; and slowing of speech, thinking, or movement. If a visitor perceives some or all of these symptoms in the resident, it will be a signal to be alert to a better understanding of what affects the resident and to better work out ways of making the visits more inspiring of hope—but not to play psychiatrist.

Treatment: A visitor's treatment of depression begins and ends in an indefatigable faith in the person's inner capacities, and the road between is called patience. Sometimes the best treatment is a listening ear that does not judge, preach, or pressure, but simply accepts. Just allowing some of the poisonous thoughts out for air can take the bite out of them. Having truly listened, the visitor will be able to determine the next move. Diatribes and complaints without end are not healthy, either, so after the airing has occurred, the visitor should try to identify the feelings that have emerged and talk about them. ("You must feel very frustrated." "You are feeling lonely because . . .")

Real interest, genuine caring, thoughtful remembrances, acute listening, and genuine acceptance can sometimes do more for a patient than psychiatric care.

Drug reactions. We are all aware that even such a simple medication as aspirin has its side effects. It comes as no surprise, then, that some of the drugs taken to ameliorate the physical and psychological illnesses among the aged would also have side effects. The purpose of informing the visitor about these effects is to create an awareness of the role of drugs as influences on mood and capacity for response in the people being visited. The small amount of information imparted here will not give us sufficient knowledge to assess the quality of drug care the residents receive.

Drug-induced side effects (extra-pyramidal manifestations) can show themselves in movement disorders which range from mild shaking to violent jerking, apathy, shuffling gait, drooling at the mouth, difficulty in swallowing, muscular rigidity, constant nervousness, inappropriate movement, and involuntary tongue and mouth movements.

It is important to know that a change in medication can alleviate some of these side effects. If medication (especially tranquilizers) has been used over a period of years, these symptoms may be irreversible.

Diabetes. This disease affects more than 10 percent of any grouping of elderly persons in long term care facilities. One doctor has said if we live long enough any one of us could contract diabetes.

Diabetes mellitus is an adult-onset diabetes that is a result of a decline in glucose tolerance level as age advances. Most of these cases of diabetes are controlled by diet, and do not include insulin as a medication. But for adults who have enjoyed the indulgence of a sweet tooth, this kind of diet change means great suffering; they need the support and encouragement of all.

Diabetes that has gotten out of control results in such tragic situations as vision loss, circulation problems (resulting often in amputations), and renal failure (kidney problems). Residents who have experienced any of these problems need special encouragement because they tend to become depressed. Often visitors can do much to build morale and to encourage residents to utilize the remaining good parts of the body—to maintain as much self-determination as possible.

Losses of hearing, sight, limbs, or bodily functions

Although most of the above problems are treated singly in the next few pages, they all have a common complication. The resident experiences the loss of a member of the body or its function as a "mini-death," and as such needs to mourn it. The visitor can do a great deal to facilitate this process by being the person with whom the resident can rant, rave, grieve, cry, and eventually bury the experience psychologically. This is an absolutely necessary stage to go through before the person can get on with the process of living well with what is left for the time that is left.

The hard of hearing.
1. Talk at a moderate rate.
2. Keep your voice at about the same volume throughout each sentence; do not drop the voice at the end of the sentence. A lower voice range is often easier to hear.
3. Always speak as clearly as possible. Distinctness does not mean shouting.
4. Make the change to a new subject, such as name, number, or unusual word, at a slower rate.
5. Watch the expression on the listener's face and note when your words are not caught. Do not repeat the whole sentence. Usually only a word or name was not clear.
6. Remember that the hard of hearing may depend to a considerable extent on reading your lips. Face them so they can see your lips as you speak.
7. Don't speak to a hard-of-hearing person abruptly. Attract his attention first by facing him and looking straight into his eyes, or by touching his hand or shoulder lightly.
8. If a person has one good ear, stand or sit on that side when talking to him. Be sure the hearing aid is in place and turned on, and check to see that the batteries are working.
9. Facial expressions are important clues to meaning. Remember that an affectionate or amused tone of voice may be lost on a hard-of-hearing person.
10. Many hard-of-hearing persons are unduly sensitive about their handicap, and will pretend to understand you when they don't. When you detect

this situation, tactfully repeat your message in different words until it gets across.

The blind or nearly blind.

1. A blind person is simply unable to see, or to see clearly. Most often such persons are bright and intelligent. They are capable of sharing in a variety of ways. Other senses are often very sharp and make the person a receptive and entertaining conversationalist.

2. Remember that many older blind patients have had sight most of their days, and are delighted to recall episodes and happenings of sighted days.

3. Blind persons love to have things described to them—the weather, new puppies, the dress you are wearing, the hobby just completed, their surroundings.

4. Blind persons love to feel things, and take great delight in shapes, contours, and textures. They are very receptive to touch, and enjoy exploring a visitor's face and hands.

5. Small things done for blind patients give them much comfort: reading mail for them, doing their hair, touching up their nails, reading stories and items from the newspaper, writing notes.

6. Blind people are not necessarily deaf, though many people find themselves shouting at them as if they were. The ears of the blind are very sensitive to sounds, and this is distressing.

7. There are many resources available to the blind:

Talking books on record and tape, as well as the machines for playing them, are available free of charge nationally. Many convalescent homes subscribe to sources for these, but need visitors to see that the records or tapes are functioning correctly or to change them.

American Bible Society, 1865 Broadway, New
York, N.Y. 10023; (212) 581-7400

American Foundation for the Blind, 15 West 16th
Street, New York, N.Y. 10011; (212) 620-
2000

Braille Institute of America, Inc., 741 North
Vermont Avenue, Los Angeles, CA 90029;
(213) 663-1111

Lighthouse for the Blind (in some locations; con-
sult telephone directory in your area)

National Library Service for the Blind and Phy-
sically Handicapped, Library of Congress,
Washington, D.C. 20540; (202) 426-5000

Narrative records are available at many libraries,
as well as *large-print books* for the partially sighted.
Most libraries also have a shut-in service; volunteers
bring the reading materials to the sick person and
return them.

Braille Bibles are available from the American
Bible Society, address above.

The stroke patient.

1. Each stroke patient is an individual, and
though the affliction shows itself in common signs,
each person responds uniquely.

2. Paralysis of one kind or another often accom-
panies the stroke. The stroke usually leaves one side
affected. When visiting such a person it is a good idea
to sit on the "good" side, since there may be damage
to the vision and hearing capabilities.

3. Find out what exercises have been recommended to the person you are visiting. The nursing
staff will inform you if the patient is not able to tell
you. Visitors can often help the stroke victim by ask-
ing him to demonstrate the exercises.

4. Certain strokes affect a person's speech and cause aphasia. This may simply cause stammering or a great difficulty in getting words out, or it may result in speech sounding like gibberish. Here are some helps:

> Let the patient struggle to get the word out. Try not to supply the word until it is absolutely necessary.
>
> Assure the patient that you want him or her to try talking.
>
> Writing the word is sometimes helpful. If this is the case bring a large pad or a blackboard.
>
> If the stroke patient cannot write, it is helpful to have pictures of common things to which he or she can point.
>
> Phrase your questions so that the aphasic person can respond with a yes or no, or a movement of the head. Start a sentence and let patient finish.
>
> Give the patient choices. This facilitates independence and helps supply the missing vocabulary. (Do you want candy or fruit?)
>
> Instead of correcting errors, restate what you think the person is trying to say.

5. Many people make the mistake of assuming that the stroke victim is senile. Very often the intelligence capacity has been unaffected, and it is particularly distressing to these individuals to be treated as confused.

6. Some stroke patients become verbally abusive, have crying jags, or exhibit other unsettling behavior. It is important to realize that the patient is not in control of this behavior and that there is nothing personal in it.

The senile and confused.

1. A greater overall sensitivity on the part of the visitor is required for confused and senile older persons.

2. Very disoriented persons may need your help in becoming aware of simple things like where they are and what day it is. The visitor should remember to state who he is each visit, and to recall things that will help the patient remember. Even if the person does not remember you each time, genuine interest and caring makes its impact on the heart regardless of a person's state of mind.

3. Senile or confused patients sometimes seem to be in a kind of unaware vacuum. A gentle touch will often bring the visitor to their attention. A touch can speak all kinds of languages and cross mental blocks and barriers.

4. Senile patients may fantasize that something terrible has happened or will happen. This can make them very anxious. Visitors can alleviate some of this anxiety by being very calm and gentle. Speak reassuringly that the person "must have had a bad dream." Sometimes it is enough just to acknowledge that they are worried and that you will help them all you can.

5. Remember that many visitors walk away from such patients, or show disgust. The visitor who accepts the person as he or she is does much to affirm good things in the individual. Most patients are not senile or confused all the time. They are aware of people's reactions.

6. Even though the person does not seem to be listening or seems incapable of understanding you, do not discuss his condition in front of him.

7. It is easy to get into the habit of talking to

senile and confused patients like children because of their condition. This is unfortunate, because they are often capable of detecting this condescension.

8. It is a temptation to "go along with" obviously impossible stories told by senile or confused persons. This only serves to increase the confusion. A visitor can say, "You must really wish your mother was alive and here with you," without putting down the person with "Your mother has been dead for 20 years."

9. Attempt to find something about the past of the senile or confused person from the staff. Senile patients often have poor memories about what happened that day, but can talk logically and clearly about events which happened fifteen years ago.

10. Visits with senile and confused patients can be made more enjoyable by bringing things to do, such as winding yarn into a ball, or pulling threads for placemats, or sorting items.

11. Visits to the senile and confused should be short, as their attention span drifts easily. It is best to visit in very small numbers, preferably one at a time, as numbers confuse the person.

The terminally ill and dying.

1. It is the experience of most counselors of the terminally ill that they know they are dying, even when family and friends are locked into secrecy over the fact. Dying people do not always share this knowledge with others. This is partly due to the fact that it is painful to think about, and they are sometimes relieved that everyone is guarding the reality. There comes a time, though, when they do want to talk about the impending death and unfinished tasks. They wish to share with an understanding person their feelings, especially the rage, anger, guilt, and isolation. The

friendly visitor who has built a bridge of caring and listening may well be the person to receive such confidences.

2. Elisabeth Kubler-Ross is an eminent psychiatrist who has done much research and teaching on death and dying. I encourage every visitor to read her book, *On Death and Dying*. The book will help you to understand your own feelings about this subject, and will enrich you with attitudes and ideas that will make any contact you may have with the dying worthwhile to you and to them. Since most of the people we visit are quite elderly, the possibility that one of your friends may die is high, and the suggestions here and in Dr. Ross's book will be helpful.

3. It is a fact that often neither physicians, nurses, friends, or family want to listen to or talk to a patient about dying, even when the fact is known to the patient. It is tempting to reach out in false assurance that "Everything is going to be O.K.," or "What do you mean you are dying—why, tomorrow you'll be up in your chair and before long out of here." If we don't rush these denials into our conversation, but allow patients to express their fears, we may give them more comfort than a thousand reassurances. This does not mean that we leave them without hope. There must always be the blue skies of tomorrow for an ill person to hope for a change or a miracle. We must support hope without denying the fears that accompany it. Dr. Ross claimed that in all her contacts with dying people, no matter what the stage of illness or coping mechanisms, each patient maintained some form of hope until the final moment.

4. Many dying people hang on to life because of unfinished business. They worry about someone being left behind with no one to take care of them. Others

are filled with guilt about real or imagined sins, and need to expiate them even if it is just to air them. It is always possible to be a listener to the latter, but the former may take a great deal of diplomacy unless you are very familiar with the family. Most convalescent homes have a social work designee. It would be wise to seek her out and share anything in the line of unfinished business that may have been shared with you.

5. Elisabeth Kubler-Ross indicates several stages on the part of the dying patient in his attitude toward death: denial and isolation, bargaining, anger, depression, and acceptance. These reactions will last for different lengths of time for different people, and can exist together or replace each other. Perhaps the most difficult of these to sense as a defense mechanism is anger. This rage can be directed at the most absurd things as well as the obvious ones of family, doctor, hospital, and so forth. The depression that sets in after the anger has subsided or alongside the anger is hardest for visitors to deal with. This is the time for listening, for hearing with the ear of the heart, and for the genuine comfort of touch. If we can communicate about death without fear, anxiety, and denial, we have opened the door to our friend who can then choose his or her own time to walk through.

6. One of our ministers to the sick reminds us that even our silent presence is important to dying people. It assures them they are still valuable.

Visiting in the home.
1. Visiting shut-ins in their home requires many of the same qualities and much of the same understanding and loving sensitivity that is needed by visitors to convalescent homes or residential care homes. Actually, visitors to the homes have an advantage

over visitors to the institutions, in that the visitee is on his or her own turf and is usually more independent.

2. In visiting shut-ins in their homes, the visitor must make sure of his or her welcome. A call-ahead method is a good plan. Usually it is best not to call too far ahead, as elderly persons and shut-ins have little else to do but anticipate visitors and pleasant events. A day or two notice will also let you know if the shut-in feels up to visitors. If this is a first visit, explain your purpose in visiting and the purpose of the group you may be associated with. Leave your name and number so that the shut-in can make any necessary changes. Secure the day and time that is acceptable, and then make every effort to be on time.

3. The length of a visit is usually determined by the health of the shut-in and how much time the visitor has. A half hour is often adequate for first visits; as a relationship develops, visits can be lengthened as sensitivity indicates. The same time of day and the same day of week makes visits much more appreciated, as they can be anticipated with the imagination and the heart. It is a good idea to leave a card with your name and phone number so that your shut-in can initiate contact with you if necessary and appropriate.

4. Any satisfying relationship has opportunities for both parties to give. If your shut-in wants to make refreshments for you or share in other small giving ways, graciously receive them. Such a way of relating helps the shut-in maintain a sense of dignity and control. If you can accept the hospitality, they are more likely to accept you and the things you might want to do for them.

5. Help shut-ins maintain and foster independence. It is best to avoid doing things for them that

they can do themselves, even if so doing puts you more at ease. It is also a temptation for visitors to want to "do over" a person's home or apartment to what we think would be more useful. Usually, careful listening will indicate if the shut-in wants anything done about the living environment, and even then any changes should be made at the shut-in's design.

    6. One veteran visitor to shut-ins has said humorously (but pointedly), "Watch out that you don't accidentally kick the bedroom slippers under the bed or out of reach." This bit of advice reminds us that we want our visit to be helpful and affirming to the shut-in. Bring a heart that feels deeply and is accepting, a mind that searches for ways of making the shut-in happier, and a sense of humor that validates the funnybone of life.

    7. Visitors to shut-ins should be attuned to what the community and church or temple offer to make the life of a home-bound person easier. There are agencies and groups that offer such aids as meals on wheels, legal aid, home health aid, medical transport, and other life-improving helps. While it may not be your job to bring such help yourself, you can put the person you visit in touch with these services.

Learning Top from Bottom[1]

5

I took my hand and placed it in that wrinkled one and
    thought—
What a lot I have to give!
What life to bring to this aged shell,
What songs to sing for this voice gone dull!
What glorious scenes of happenings to paint for the
    eyes so dim!
What fleet-footed dances to prance around these un-
    steady sluggish feet!
What goodness from my bounty to lavish upon this
    helpless one!
What giving I planned to grace the days of this
    burned-out receiver!
What unfettered independence would pluck wild
    flowers for this dependent one!
And I heard—wait—
You there, gutted with the smugness of well-being,
What do you know of nights without end, pain without
    release, desertion without surcease?

1. The book *Aging: The Fulfillment of Life* by H. J. M.
Nouwen and W. J. Gaffney (Garden City, N. Y.: Doubleday &
Co., Inc., 1974; Image Books, 1976) inspired this poem.

What will you say in your glibness to the wall of a
        mind that has shut down from weariness, or
        uselessness, or whys no longer asking for
        answers.
What can you add to the minutes of life slipping away
        from a fight long finished?
What song will relieve the keenly felt sense of burden-
        someness?
What dance will lighten the hours on end spent alone
        without purpose?
What kind of tomorrow can your eyes describe for the
        one who shudders in the weak sun of yester-
        day's memories?
Looking closely, I understood.
The truth was not to be found in either of our visions
        alone.
That wrinkled shell has more than darkness to shout
        about!
        More than loneliness to wrap about thin shoulders,
        More than pain has coursed through those bones!
Those lips have drunk long and fully from the cup
        of life and have known songs and dances
        and thrills I'll never touch.
That wondrous mind has filtered through countless
        experiences and distilled life's real meaning
        —what's worth dancing for, and what isn't;
What little can be held tightly in one's hands,
        and what unbounded treasures can be stored
        in one's heart!
This incredible person knows what I have not dis-
        cerned well yet: that life is not determined
        by what we do, or have—not even by our
        friends, relatives, and loved ones—and is lit
        from the heart.

This wizened one knows—though between us we may
have to unearth the knowledge—that it is
not awards, degrees, presidentships that
confirm life, but being in touch with the
spirit within, living with the love-energy of
that spirit, and comfortable in the solitude
sifting from its end-day.

So this aging one takes my hand and teaches me what
a lot life has to give, and us to each other.

What songs to trust, life remembered and looked for-
ward to, we can harmonize together!

What a dance our combined feet can trace on the
years left to both of us!

How else will I learn top from bottom except from this
long-term life-maker?

I know why this old tree was left—
so that I might sit in its shadow and not
forget the preciousness of life each moment!

Sister Pat Murphy, O.L.V.M.